Poems From Scotland

Edited By Sarah Olivo

First published in Great Britain in 2018 by:

Young Writers
Remus House
Coltsfoot Drive
Peterborough
PE2 9BF
Telephone: 01733 890066
Website: www.youngwriters.co.uk

All Rights Reserved
Book Design by Ashley Janson
© Copyright Contributors 2018
SB ISBN 978-1-78896-470-8
Printed and bound in the UK by BookPrintingUK
Website: www.bookprintinguk.com
YB0358T

FOREWORD

Welcome, Reader, to *Rhymecraft - Poems From Scotland*.

Among these pages you will find a whole host of poetic gems, built from the ground up by some wonderful young minds. Included are a variety of poetic styles, from amazing acrostics to creative cinquains, from dazzling diamantes to fascinating free verse.

Here at Young Writers our objective has always been to help children discover the joys of poetry and creative writing. Few things are more encouraging for the aspiring writer than seeing their own work in print. We are proud that our anthologies are able to give young authors this unique sense of confidence and pride in their abilities as well as letting their poetry reach new audiences.

The editing process was a tough but rewarding one that allowed us to gain an insight into the blooming creativity of today's primary school pupils. I hope you find as much enjoyment and inspiration in the following poetry as I have, so much so that you pick up a pen and get writing!

Sarah Olivo

CONTENTS

Currie Primary School, Currie

Abbey Weller (10)	1
Emma Jo Buchan (10)	2
Jack Mackenzie (10)	4
Fraya Gentle (10)	5
Seth Hill-Cousins (11)	6
Aimee Margaret Brown (10)	7
Leah Anne Cummings Douglas (10)	8
Xavier Unis (11)	9
Amy Sutherland (10)	10
Maryam Shahid (10)	11
Harrison Mackenzie (10)	12
Caitlyn Leah Gray (10)	13
Alex Krzyzanowski (10)	14
Thomas Alexander (10)	15
Artie Pearce (10)	16
Fatma Ali Said (10)	18
Cameron Miller (10)	19
Julia Kamyk (10)	20
Sam Stachan (10)	21
Katie Buchan (10)	22
Hamish Scott (10)	23
Isla Scott (10)	24
Isla Galbraith (10)	25
Emma Anderson (10)	26
Grace Quinn (11)	27
Emily Flower (10)	28
Isaac Clarke (10)	29
Sana Dean (10)	30
Imogen Cook (10)	31
Katie Rogers (10)	32
Finlay John Simon (11)	33
Isla Wilson (10)	34
Moray MacLennan (10)	35
Isobel Lewis (10)	36
Stephanie-Anne Mccauley (10)	37
Sandy Bishop (10)	38
Bella Hanley (10)	39
Charlie Lois Vaughan (10)	40
Ewen William Peter Browning (10)	41
Natalia Iwan (11)	42
Ryan Mclellan (10)	43

Daviot Primary School, Inverness

Katie Elder (10)	44
Maree MacAskill (10)	45
Lucy Hunter (9)	46
Archie Bone (10)	47
Evie Henderson (9)	48
Ellie Henderson (9)	49
Kirsten Kortland (9)	50
Lucca Williams (10)	51
Joshua Evason (9)	52
Angus Cameron (8)	53
Ethan Parker (10)	54

Glencoats Primary School, Paisley

Charlie Ellingham (11)	55
Amy Kate Higgins (11)	56

Gourdon Primary School, Gourdon

Izzie Kemlo (8)	57
Sam Oag (9)	58
Kiera Elizabeth Dunn (9)	60
Isla Oag (7)	62
Zak Boydell (9)	63

Darren Hamilton-Hall (9)	64
Erin Fraser (9)	66
Olivia Newlands (9)	67
Charlotte Olivia Morris (7)	68
Anna Hamilton-Hall (7)	69
Murray Watt (7)	70

Greenhill Primary School, Coatbridge

Brooke Donna McCarroll (11)	71
Faye Morgan (11)	72
Grace O'Neill (11)	74
Arran MacInnes (11)	76
Ethan Fleming (11)	78
Kyle Sedgeworth (11)	79
Harry Burns (11)	80
Anaru Maika MacDougall (11)	81

Harestanes Primary School, Kirkintilloch

Andrew Stewart (8)	82

Helmsdale Primary School, Helmsdale

Luke Stephen Ainsworth (10)	83
Grace McConnach (11)	84
Danielle Cowie (10)	85
Ashli Hope (11)	86
Lawlyn Grant (10)	87
Helen Grace Turner (11)	88
Rhys Keith (10)	89
Millie Wood (10)	90

Heriot Primary School, Heriot

Holly Reid (11)	91
Daisy Hilton (11)	92
Flynn Walker (10)	93
Aaron Willis (11)	94
Sam Fletcher (11)	95
Sofia Pirone (9)	96
Louella King (10)	97

High Mill Primary School, Carluke

Eilidh Christine Kerr (10)	98
Becky Williamson (10)	100
Leahmarie Martin (11)	101
Aiden Isik (11)	102
David Connacher (11)	103
Oliver Isik (10)	104
Jasmin Todd (11)	105

Inverallochy School, Inverallochy

Matthew Sim (9)	106
Katie Crockett (10)	107
Cameron Ritchie (10)	108
Monique Ritchie (10)	109
Katie Noble (9)	110
Emily Claire Marie Stephen (10)	111
Nathan Novell-Frazer (10)	112
Caleb Howe (10)	113

The High School Of Glasgow, Bearsden

Nimrita Kaur Samra (9) & Eva Jean Stirling	114
Maya Marshall (9) & Hannah Eve Reilly (9)	115
Chloe Kirk (8) & Rosie Snedden	116

THE POEMS

Crystal Cliffs

C old and unforgiving stand the high mountains,
R ed blood has stained their mighty structures, though the horror has yet to end,
Y our soul will surely succumb to the terror and the pain,
S taring deep into your soul, the moon eerily hangs unmoving in the sky,
T he Crystal watches as her soul destroys what she loved and cherished,
A ll the pain, fear and loss were poured into the mountains,
L ilac colours dance in and out of the portal, twisting together in a poisonous harmony.

C loaking itself in a silvery mist,
L ocked deep in the heart of the mountains are fear, pain and terror,
I solated are the mountains, fearing her destruction,
F oreboding and trapped is the evil mountain range,
F orever alone, the Crystal turns to hate,
S o hate will be her very last breath.

Abbey Weller (10)
Currie Primary School, Currie

Imagination Land

I magination Land is where people go to be happy,
M ermaids, mermen, unicorns, fairies, pirates and tons more fascinating creatures to discover,
A mazing things that you can learn about them,
G irls normally hang out at the mall and boys normally hang out at the basketball court or the football stadium,
I reland, Scotland, China, Japan - these are some of the places where people imagine going to,
N ice people love fighting for good,
A mazing adventures that take you to places that you never imagined,
T errific things happen,
I f you are a good person in Imagination Land, they will accept you,
O rdinary people that don't believe never get to come in here,
N everland is a great place the play in peace.

L earn a lot about them,
A ny time, there can
N ever be a lie, because lying is bad,
D iscoveries here are extraordinary.

Emma Jo Buchan (10)
Currie Primary School, Currie

Infection World

I t cannot be the world - it is as dark as space,
N ever would a human dream of this dust ball,
F eeble buildings everywhere, some destroyed,
E scaping seems impossible from the monsters,
C reeping through gaps as grey as stone,
T wisting building creaking in the wind,
I n all buildings lies nothing apart from blood and wood,
O ld, locked and abandoned, the world looks decrepit, it feels alone,
N ot looking like the world - it looks like a dump.

W hite is no longer a colour; only black, grey and brown,
O nly us and the undead, they're as fast as snails,
R avaging through flesh, bone and skin,
L ike rotting food, it's petrifying,
D estructive monsters destroying the world.

Jack Mackenzie (10)
Currie Primary School, Currie

Unicorn Land

U nicorns dance on rainbows, elegantly in the sun.
N ormally their magic is strong, but some unicorns are born weak.
I ce unicorns' manes are as white as snow covering up the trees.
C andy falling down from the sky, it lands on the unicorns.
O riginal unicorns only have ten powers, but others have lots more.
R unning like the wind, the unicorns dart all over Unicorn Land.
N ight and day, they fly through the sky, their coats glittering.

L oving and cute the baby unicorns are when they're born.
A fter eating their magical dinner, they go to sleep.
N apping silently through the night in their cosy beds.
D o you believe in unicorns?

Fraya Gentle (10)
Currie Primary School, Currie

Alien Sea Life World

A lien sea life rules this world
L ush green plants in these waters
I n the depths, you better be safe - otherwise, you will
E nd up dead
N ever seen again.

S ubtle it may be
E normous too
A nd don't let that fool you, or you will end up being food.

L ean over the boat
I f you dare, you will
F ind yourself super scared
E aten by a creature, then who's to blame?

W hether you're on a boat
O r swimming
R emember that you're not the only one there - so don't be
L oud or you will end up
D ead.

Seth Hill-Cousins (11)
Currie Primary School, Currie

In Your Head

D reams can come true,
R abbits made of sugar,
E lephants made of candyfloss,
A nd candy canes.
M any fairies live here,
S mall as ants.

V ans as tiny as crumbs,
S ilent as the wind.

N ow we are talking about the dark side.
I n the night, they rise:
G oblins in the house down the street.
H ere we have vampires,
T aking blood from every soul in sight.
M r Demon running his evil shop.
A re you willing to go to this land?
R eady to suck blood, the vampires wait.
E very day, the trolls meet.
S caryland.

Aimee Margaret Brown (10)
Currie Primary School, Currie

The Land Of Food

T his land is mouthwatering,
H ills made out of mud pie,
E verything here is food.

L amp posts made out of Cheestrings,
A pples with sweet, sticky and succulent caramel,
N ew flavours of food every day,
D inners made in boiling hot ovens.

O lives made to look like jelly beans,
F inished plates that have been eaten by ravenous children.

F ood everybody loves to eat,
O n Christmas day, succulent turkey is eaten,
O bviously on Easter, everyone eats eggs with delights,
D ogs gobbling up bonbons and getting blue around their mouths.

Leah Anne Cummings Douglas (10)
Currie Primary School, Currie

Hell Down Below

H appiness you will never see here
E vil lurking around every corner
L eaving this place will be your worst nightmare
L egend - that's what people may think of this place.

D emons possessing your soul
O pportunistic danger everywhere
W arning, danger, danger!
N ever ever see happy things.

B elow the surface, something lurks down deep
E vil monsters you may see
L ord Velum of Hell ruling
O ver all the monsters (the smaller, the deadlier)
W ild beasts feeding on the fear of the living.

Xavier Unis (11)
Currie Primary School, Currie

Movie World

M ovies like The Greatest Showman, Coco, all good things
O n a sugar rush because you've eaten too much popcorn
V igorously loud movies playing through the ninety-foot screens
I ce Blasts, strawberry, blue raspberry - the best drinks ever
E ven better than watching a boring movie on the television.

W orld of popcorn and delicious treats
O deon, Cineworld, Movie Land is better
R unning around crazy because you're so excited
L oving it like it's a tiny baby
D ying, because you desperately want to go there.

Amy Sutherland (10)
Currie Primary School, Currie

Animal Land

Animal land is a mysterious place
Nobody knows where Animal Land is placed
It seems like it's as big as Spain
With galloping horses eating hay!

Cheeky squirrels in the trees
Gigantic giraffes eating leaves
Rabbits and bunnies hopping along
With their brand-new squeaky song!

There are a lot of mountains in this land
A lot of them are filled with sand
There are a lot of flowers here
Most of them have petals shaped like ears!

Every animal is happy here
With their brand-new pairs of ears
All of them can listen
Without hesitation!

Maryam Shahid (10)
Currie Primary School, Currie

Football Land

Stadiums as high as Mount Everest,
Hundreds of thousands of seats,
Never-ending experiences,
These are the stadiums.

Flying as fast as sound are footballs,
Shining in the completely black sky,
Players fighting for the ball,
Millions of footballs.

As rich as Saudi Arabia,
As popular as America in the summer,
Millions of fans of football,
This is the meaning of fun.

Surprises happen no one thought would,
Kits, flags, scarves, it has it all,
Holding up trophies, celebrating with your fans,
This is the meaning of life.

Harrison Mackenzie (10)
Currie Primary School, Currie

Gymnastics Land

G ymnastics is a wonderful sport,
Y oung to old can do it,
M agical skills to learn,
N othing you can't learn,
A mazing competitions to win at,
S omersaults and twists,
T ons of sparkly leotards,
I nteresting competitions when someone makes a mistake,
C limbing the ropes to get strength,
S it in the splits to get flexible.

L and of fun and joy,
A mazing gymnasts for you to meet,
N o athlete you can't meet,
D oor to your life.

Caitlyn Leah Gray (10)
Currie Primary School, Currie

Portal To Darkness

P ortal to complete hell,
O n the lookout is a beast,
R elease the beast and everyone will die,
T otal darkness everywhere,
A lways stay alert, or you'll be dead,
L urking is a killer creature.

T ry to survive,
O r you'll be history.

D arkness rules,
A pply or you will die,
R ace through the darkness,
K iller is,
N ever explored,
E xplore the mysterious,
S urvival is key,
S tay out!

Alex Krzyzanowski (10)
Currie Primary School, Currie

Candy Cream Land

C hildren, hyper
A fter a sugar rush
N ever-ending ice cream, cold, sticky, brr!
D ay after day of swallowing sweets
Y um!

C ones as big as the Eiffel Tower
R efreshing milkshakes
E very sweet you ask for
A ppears in front of you
M any different flavours for you to choose.

L and of sweets and ice cream
A huge chocolate fountain filled with strawberries
N ow we've eaten too much; we burst and we've
D ied.

Thomas Alexander (10)
Currie Primary School, Currie

Candy Land

You will see no bricks,
peanut butter makes them stick,
it all makes you sick,
but you want to stay for a bit.

It's all so fun,
dancing in the strawberry sun,
houses made of chips,
no bricks or sticks.

No blocks,
no rocks,
just Jelly Tots,
it rains sweets,
but not as treats.

Logs are still brown,
but don't make you frown,
as they are chocolate.

Stars still glisten,
but with sugar they shine

all so fine,
in Candy Land.
Artie Pearce (10)
Currie Primary School, Currie

The Land Of The Devil

Everlasting ferns dig into your soul,
There's no way in or out, so leave that alone,
You shall never come out alive,
The Devil shall come for you on the count of five,
Rivers of blood meander through this land,
Never accept a devil's hand.

There's a devil wearing a marvellous crown,
It's as creepy as a basement,
And it's as murderous as a clown,
Nobody there dares to make a statement,
It is the land of the Devil, so just stay away,
It's not the right place to stay.

Fatma Ali Said (10)
Currie Primary School, Currie

Candy Land

C andy everywhere, sweets covering you from head to toe
A mazing sweets, from candy canes to chocolate rivers
N o one is ever not hungry, yum!
D oughnuts are the best part, making your mouth water
Y ou will like it, everything's made out of candy!

L ike this land, care for it and the sweets are yours
A nd tons of ice cream and Celebrations
N ew sweets to discover during your journey
D o you like candy and sweets? This is the place for you!

Cameron Miller (10)
Currie Primary School, Currie

Star Of Infinity

There was a time when there was peace,
Under the star - monster had feasts,
Every monster had their role,
And their own pure monster soul.
But soon, the side of evil came,
All monsters were in deep pain,
A human with a soul of hate,
The monsters were to face their fate.
Who would they kill, who'd they trust?
Would they all just turn to dust?
Every monster had their role,
And their own cursed monster soul.
For now it is the end of war,
This is the tale of Infinity Star.

Julia Kamyk (10)
Currie Primary School, Currie

Prison Land

P rison as huge as the Empire State Building,
R eady to catch anyone escaping out.
I nside, no fun allowed.
S ometimes, people flee out of Prison Land,
O ften, people are never let out.
N o one messes with the police here.

L egs get amputated so no one escapes,
A lso, people who go to this land are automatically prisoners.
N o one dares step near this land,
D ead, they will become.

Sam Stachan (10)
Currie Primary School, Currie

Squishy Land

S atisfying wonder,
Q uick and slow rising,
U nique in their own ways,
I f you trip over, you'll be okay,
S eems like you're on a bouncy castle,
H ouses are fun to live in,
Y ou can't climb trees because they will bend over.

L and of happiness,
A nimals and people are real,
N ever get stressed out,
D on't regret living there, because you're lucky.

Katie Buchan (10)
Currie Primary School, Currie

Animal Land

A mazing creatures, tall and small
N obody's sad, so come on
I nto Animal Land!
M any strange and wonderful things happen in
A nimal Land, everything is cool in Animal
L and!

L egendary beasts, beautiful beings and many more
A wesomely fun with everything you want
N obody gets mad, we party all
D ay and into the night - you will really love it here in Animal Land.

Hamish Scott (10)
Currie Primary School, Currie

Eat Sweet Candy

E at sweet candy,
A lways very handy,
T asty Magic Stars.

S o high like Mars,
W e eat them all the time,
E veryone's like, "They're mine!"
E at sweet candy,
T otally not unhandy.

C andy tastes so good,
A nd it definitely should,
N erds and gummies,
D ark chocolate's very yummy,
Y um, yum, yum in my tummy.

Isla Scott (10)
Currie Primary School, Currie

Happy Land

Happy Land is somewhere fun
Nothing boring is ever done
Trees grow free money
And I'm not being funny.

Every time a bird tweets
It swoops down and gives you sweets
You can see people smile
When they're running a mile.

Nobody falls out
When they're messing about
Everybody's happy
Nobody is snappy.

So please come to this land,
When you need a helping hand.

Isla Galbraith (10)
Currie Primary School, Currie

Rainbow Land

R ed and blue are colours they can be,
A ll unicorns are there, night and day,
I t's a magical land,
N o other land is better,
B right colours like the sun,
O range is on the rainbow,
W hen it's raining and sunny, a rainbow appears.

L ovely like flowers,
A ll are beautiful,
N othing is better than rainbows,
D on't hate them.

Emma Anderson (10)
Currie Primary School, Currie

The Land Of Fire And Ice

In the land of fire and ice
No one there is really nice
All the people who live there
Are not really fair.

Everyone there tries to be right
Even though it ends in a fight
Someone from an ice flow - a knight
But someone from fire made a light.

In the land of fire and ice
We know no one's really nice
Fire and ice don't get along
So let's all go and say, "So long."

Grace Quinn (11)
Currie Primary School, Currie

Mansion Money Land

Mansion Money Land has lots of hero horses,
We feed them with honey,
Definitely not money!
The land is so rich, no problems come our way,
No horses ever say nay!

The hero horses save people from their money problems,
But now there're no more!
What's the point of living in,
A stable behind a door?
What shall we do?

We could make a problem!
Should we, or should we not?

Emily Flower (10)
Currie Primary School, Currie

Wonky Hill

W here the wonkiness is unreal,
O n a wonky hill,
N o normal person dares,
K illing is illegal there,
Y et people still kill.

H ills are normally cone shape, but this hill is zigzagging,
I t has all different shapes and sizes,
L olapre is the alien language they speak,
L iterally, they will kill you if you come too close.

Isaac Clarke (10)
Currie Primary School, Currie

Sweetie Land

This land is Sweetie Land,
The people here are gingerbread men,
They are all ages from zero to ten,
They play just like you,
Except they draw with lollipop pens.

The grass is one really long pencil,
The whole world is made out of sweeties,
You don't have to go to a shop and pay at a till,
You can eat all the sweets you want here,
There won't be a single tear.

Sana Dean (10)
Currie Primary School, Currie

Fairy Land

F luttering up so high in the sky
A ctually like a butterfly
I nvestigating right above the land
R ight where any fairy can understand
Y ou would love it there, indeed.

L ively fairies all around
A nd they don't even make a sound.
N aughty little fairies all around.
D o you believe in fairies? I do, I do!

Imogen Cook (10)
Currie Primary School, Currie

Candy Land

C andy canes hanging everywhere you go
A ero bubbles bubbling away
N erds raining from Candy Castle
D ark chocolate raining down
Y orkie dropping down the candy mountain.

L ollipop sticks sticking in the ground
A strobelt hanging on the tree
N utella pods wherever you can see
D ip Dab, all the sugar you can see.

Katie Rogers (10)
Currie Primary School, Currie

Fearth

Fearth is
the backup world
for humans
every superhero lives there.

Earth is dying
and the humans
have to leave Earth
and move to Fearth.

No humans must be
on Earth anymore
Reach to Fearth
they must.

Time for Earth
to blow up.
Home is gone.
Time for a new beginning!

Finlay John Simon (11)
Currie Primary School, Currie

Cloud Land

C razy shapes
L and of happiness
O n a bright summer's day, the clouds go away
U nicorns like to dance on them
D ancing on them is fun, as well as eating them.

L ovely village
A nd amazing parks
N obody hates them
D on't eat the humans, eat the clouds.

Isla Wilson (10)
Currie Primary School, Currie

Reblux Land

R obbing banks, jewellery stores and trains
E xcellent getaway cars
B arging things out of the way
L ife of taking risks
U nlimited car respawning
X -class cars.

L iving the dream
A nd motorbikes
N atural dream
D riving like a boss.

Moray MacLennan (10)
Currie Primary School, Currie

Ocean's Heart

O ver a wave I go
C rashing over them
E legantly, I soar away
A way I hide in the sea
N ot coming out
S wim down and come see.

H eavenly, unique
E asily found by fakes
A m red as can be
R are to see
T ry to find me.

Isobel Lewis (10)
Currie Primary School, Currie

Love Land

L ove is a beautiful feeling,
O riginal, kind men want you,
V ery romantic life,
E lves do a show for you to have fun.

L ove is magical,
A touch of love changes your life,
N ever let yourself down,
D arling, you're in love now.

Stephanie-Anne Mccauley (10)
Currie Primary School, Currie

Battle Land

In Battle Land, it is war,
And there is no exit door,
Everybody revives,
Into some other lives,
And they spawn in a random team,
And sometimes it's mean,
Being put in a high division,
But sometimes it's nice,
But with a good group,
You're walking on thin ice.

Sandy Bishop (10)
Currie Primary School, Currie

The Dream

T he candy castle
H at store is the best because they are
E dible, caps made of gobstoppers.

D rops of jam fall off the trees
R ain is gumdrops, yum
E dible work sheets
A ir raids flying in the sky
M oon made out of a gumball.

Bella Hanley (10)
Currie Primary School, Currie

Giraffes

G reat, gorgeous creatures
I ntelligent, imaginative things
R umbling through Africa
A mazing, adorable faces
F abulous and famous animals
F illed with light and love
E xcellent brown spots
S uper bright and playful.

Charlie Lois Vaughan (10)
Currie Primary School, Currie

Happy Land

Happy Land is not bland
Instead it's rather grand
Everyone lends a helping hand.

It's a land of fun
For everyone
Underneath our wonder, the sun.

Have fun here
Without any fear
It's only fun and cheer.

Ewen William Peter Browning (10)
Currie Primary School, Currie

Cupcake Land
A haiku poem

Children having fun,
Cupcake cars are whooshing by,
The dream place to be.

Natalia Iwan (11)
Currie Primary School, Currie

The Zombie Apocalypse Land
A haiku poem

Murderous and mean.
They are quite easy to kill.
It is too scary.

Ryan Mclellan (10)
Currie Primary School, Currie

Dragonite

The tiny tortoises always team up,
to break the speed record.
You can hear them chittering round,
the crunchy chocolate river!
The lizards laugh,
at the dangerous dragons.
My flying drone,
always moans.

All of the giggling goats,
sail away in my big boats.
The silly snakes say, "Hooray!" all day,
why won't they go away?

Dragonite is such a big place,
we always float around in space!
The food is always really good,
you might get your food half-chewed,
from the cow that just mooed.
You can come...
as long as you bring food!

Katie Elder (10)
Daviot Primary School, Inverness

The Animal World!

Welcome to my Animal World!

There was a fluffy grey goat,
who jumped in a submarine boat.
Mr Fox climbed up the rocks,
and in his jaws were a pair of socks.

Once, there was a cow called Daisy,
she was just a little lazy.
She lay on her bed, scratching her head,
and phoned her friend called Maisy.

With the spectacular snakes,
are the dark blue lakes.
And the monkeys ate,
the brilliant banana cakes.

There was a bird,
that said he heard,
a poem all about,
the Animal World!

Maree MacAskill (10)
Daviot Primary School, Inverness

Candy Land

Welcome to my Candy Land!
Where happiness is the only strand,
With candy canes for the trees,
And sweet grass up to your knees,
You will be pleased.

Sweet treats you can eat,
Come sit by the beach,
With a chocolate lake by your feet.

Gummy fish will be swimming by,
Chocolate birds in the sky,
Flying very, very high.
Oh my, oh my, oh my!
You will never say goodbye.

So why don't you give it a try?

Lucy Hunter (9)
Daviot Primary School, Inverness

Shinty City

S hinty City has it all,
H ave forty winks in a bed of sticks,
I n the city, there is McSticks with tasty food,
N o belters, only wallops for shots,
T raining in a huge stadium every day,
Y ou will be safe when you land.

C olours are yellow, black and red,
I n the city, it is always cool,
T hroughout the night, games are played,
Y ou might drive a ball car.

Archie Bone (10)
Daviot Primary School, Inverness

Animal Land

In Animal Land, there are helpful, friendly animals.
Once a month, they host,
the most wonderful ball,
in a huge hall!

They mostly run,
and have lots of great fun.
The dolphins enjoy a swim,
with their boss called Jim.

Animal Land is so much fun,
all the animals enjoy the sun.
Why don't you come visit and see?
Perhaps you will find the wallaby!

Evie Henderson (9)
Daviot Primary School, Inverness

Happy Land

Welcome to my lovely land,
where you will see lots of strawberry sand.
Treats that taste so sweet,
this place is really neat!

There stands a castle on the sand,
that is built with treats and sweets.
Superheroes protect the land,
where anyone bad will be banned.

Come and visit my happy land,
and hear the fabulous fish band!

Ellie Henderson (9)
Daviot Primary School, Inverness

A Magical Land!

Welcome to my Magical Land,
It's beautiful and grand,
Half is cold and half is warm,
In the sun, there grows a lot of corn.

In this land, the animals talk,
Rabbits, horses, birds and the croc,
With lollipop trees and sparkling rainbows,
Where will you go?

Towards the glistening snow,
Or the sunny green meadows?

Kirsten Kortland (9)
Daviot Primary School, Inverness

Sweetie Land

S weeties every square inch,
W onderful smell everywhere,
E ating amazing ice cream from the river,
E dible soil is caramel and tiny green jelly bean grass!
T he Giant Jellymen roam the world!
I had a mind-blowing experience there!
E verything is edible, so stuff your face!

Lucca Williams (10)
Daviot Primary School, Inverness

Narnia

N arnia, a place where man is king
A ll of Narnia is filled with dwarfs
R unning centaurs hunt in the woods
N arnia! Narnia! A place of talking beasts
I n their homes, badgers stay, until...
A slan! Aslan! The most high king of all - the great lion!

Joshua Evason (9)
Daviot Primary School, Inverness

Gun City Game

G uns everywhere!
U nder the lake, you can find guns galore!
N o hating war or you will be executed!

C olours are dark!
I like war!
T uesday is war day!
Y esterday is training day!

Angus Cameron (8)
Daviot Primary School, Inverness

The Animal Reef

Welcome to my spectacular land,
where you see a lot of sand.
Jump on a boat,
with a fluffy green goat.
Watch the bright blue snake,
flow down like a lake.
And see the big brown dog,
living in the bog.

Ethan Parker (10)
Daviot Primary School, Inverness

Scream Valley

H is for Halloween, the time of year you go door to door for sweets without getting into trouble.
A is for the apples you dunk for at Halloween parties.
L is for looking forward to see if any other doors will open.
L is for laughing at the jokes others tell.
O is for only eating the sweets you like.
W is for wandering the streets at night.
E is for enjoying the night out.
E is for ending the night with answering the door to others.
N is for not knowing where to hide the last of the sweets.

Charlie Ellingham (11)
Glencoats Primary School, Paisley

Family Tie

F amily means the world to me
A lways there for you
M y mum means everything to me
I love my family
L ove is in your family always
Y ou will always be loved.

Amy Kate Higgins (11)
Glencoats Primary School, Paisley

Rainforest Ville

I am a soft, shifting river
I wonder what's above my edge?
I hear birds chirping
I wish someone would notice me
I am a soft, shifting river.

I am a tall, swaying tree
I wonder what's under me?
I hear rabbits jumping
I wish I knew what was under me
I am a tall, swaying tree.

I am a slithering snake
I wonder what's for lunch?
I hear a mouse
I wish it would come near me
I am a slithering snake.

We are the rainforest
We hear people
We wonder what's out of our forest
We wish we could see
We are the rainforest.

Izzie Kemlo (8)
Gourdon Primary School, Gourdon

Arachnidville

I am a tall old tree
I wonder how many arachnids are near me
I hear them squealing and screeching
I wish they would not scuttle over me
I am a tall old tree.

I am a wide, still lake
I wonder who lives in my depths
I hear spiders slurping me up
I wish there were no droughts
I am a wide, still lake.

I am a strong scorpion
I wonder what's for lunch?
I see scorpions wrestling
I wish lunch would hurry up!
I am a strong scorpion.

I am a small fern
I wonder who lives within my leaves
I hear scorpions crunching lunch
I wish someone would notice me
I am a small fern.

I am a sneaky spider
I wonder who I'll catch today?
I hear the wind blowing
I wish there were more flies
I am a sneaky spider.

Together, we are Arachnidville
We wonder what other worlds there are
We hear the plants swaying in the wind
We look over a desert where more of us lurk
We wish we weren't cannibals
Together, we are Arachnidville.

Sam Oag (9)
Gourdon Primary School, Gourdon

Puppiesville

When you enter Puppiesville
with love, your heart will fill.
It tastes like sugar
sweet and delightful.
It looks playful and fun
fluffy like a fresh bun.
It sounds like squeaking and whining puppies
running around in the sun.
It feels like a soft and fluffy coat
as soft as a cloud afloat.
When you enter Puppiesville
with love, your heart will fill.

When you enter Puppiesville
with love your heart will fill.
It tastes like a candyland
as sweet as candyfloss.
It looks like puppies are running
and having an adventure.
It sounds like Mum and Dad barking
trying to protect their puppies.

It feels loving, caring and magical
it's puppies and dogs caring.
When you enter Puppiesville
with love, your heart will fill.

Kiera Elizabeth Dunn (9)
Gourdon Primary School, Gourdon

Deep Sea World

D iving dolphins in the distant deep.
E very creature has endlessly exciting days.
E veryone loves looking at the swimming fish.
P opping bubbles of the paddling porpoises.

S pecial shiny shells are stuck in the sand.
E els slither with slime on the slippery rock.
A n amazing Atlantic all for us to see.

W aves are crashing in the water.
O n the waves are seagulls, screeching.
R ocks are covered in slippery seaweed.
L isten to whales singing.
D ucks sometimes bob down to get fish.

Isla Oag (7)
Gourdon Primary School, Gourdon

Saturnsville

Saturnsville is lost in space.
Saturnsville looks like aliens with enormous black eyes.
Saturnsville tastes like crunchy dry toast.
Saturnsville sounds like laughing aliens having fun.
Saturnsville smells like stuffy air.

Saturnsville is lost in space.
Saturnsville looks like a massive planet with stars in the background.
Saturnsville tastes like bright yellow cheese.
Saturnsville sounds like aliens having grown-up chats.
Saturnsville is as hot as the sun.
Saturnsville smells like dirty old space rocks.

Saturnsville is lost in space.

Zak Boydell (9)
Gourdon Primary School, Gourdon

Orca Land

When I'm on my computer
creating Orca Land
my imagination can run wild.

I can hear the waves
it is an endless ocean
but it's only in my head.

I know it's only
in my head.

I can hear orcas using echolocation
it is a dream come true
but it's only in my head.

I know it's only
in my head.

I can hear orcas crying
it is a sorrowful tune
but it's only in my head.

I know it's only
in my head.

When I'm on my computer
my imagination can run wild.

Darren Hamilton-Hall (9)
Gourdon Primary School, Gourdon

Ice Cream Land

Ice Cream Land is sweet
and delicious
It tastes like cherry
and marshmallow
Ice cream is saucy
and yummy.

Ice Cream Land is colourful
and bright
Sometimes it rains
chocolate sauce
drippy and creamy
It looks like lots of
ice cream sundaes
Ice cream land feels
cold and wet.

Ice Cream Land sounds
like laughing and giggling
and children eating
and having fun.

Erin Fraser (9)
Gourdon Primary School, Gourdon

Blue Planet

My planet
is an underwater world.

It tastes like
fresh and
salty water.

It looks like
a beautiful
water wonderland.

It sounds like
starfish walking and fish frolicking
through the deep waters.

It feels like
a bunch of water guns spraying
every part of you.

Olivia Newlands (9)
Gourdon Primary School, Gourdon

Deep Sea

D olphins diving in the sea.
E very creature has a home.
E very fish is swimming around.
P recious porpoise paddling around.

S uper special shiny starfish swimming in.
E verything is shimmering and shining.
A lot of shiny shells glitter on the sand.

Charlotte Olivia Morris (7)
Gourdon Primary School, Gourdon

Deep Sea World

D olphins diving in the deep
E very dolphin is swimming and leaping
E ach day, I watch the dolphins play
P orpoises paddle along the sand.

S creeching seagulls swoop
E very shiny shell washes up
A nother day at the seaside.

Anna Hamilton-Hall (7)
Gourdon Primary School, Gourdon

The Sea

D iving deep are the dolphins
E very fish is swimming and darting
E verything is silent and lonely
P eaceful, precious and pearly.

S pecial salty world under the sea
E verything is exciting, we see
A world of adventure.

Murray Watt (7)
Gourdon Primary School, Gourdon

Animal Kingdom

Animal Kingdom is the place to be
with all the dogs barking
and the birds in the trees.

They're all friendly, "So don't be afraid
and you will love them too,"
the parrot said.

The cats with their whiskers
and the squirrels hugging their nuts
the horses peacefully sleeping in their wooden huts
and my granny from Scotland with her wee hairy mutt.

When I go to visit her
the dog barks like crazy.
On the farm, the pigs in the mud
are so lazy.

Brooke Donna McCarroll (11)
Greenhill Primary School, Coatbridge

Mythical Creature Land

The unicorns are so big and majestic
with their sparkly, fluffy wings.
They are colourful and bold with soft coats
and their magical horns can do wonderful things.

The dragons are so big and so fierce
with their shiny and amazing scales.
All the colours galore, from red to gold
but the best things of all are their big spiky tails.

Noo we are doon in Scotland
what magical creatures happen to be here?
Och aye, the Loch Ness Monster
so watch out - she could be near!

Now we are in the sky
where the speedy pegasuses soar.
But watch out for the dragon's cave
because, trust me, he will give a mighty roar.

Now we are under the deep blue sea
where the pretty mermaids swim.

With all the little sea creatures
a sweet little song they sing.

Even if you don't believe
no, I am not upset.
But I think they are all so very real
even if I haven't see them yet.

Faye Morgan (11)
Greenhill Primary School, Coatbridge

Fantasy Land

Fairies and elves are running around
If they run too far, they could be found
Unicorns and Pegasus are flying up high
Soon their babies will learn to fly.

Dragons and monsters roaring out fire
Whilst birds and insects fly up higher
Mermaids swimming in the magical ocean
While witches and wizards are testing potions.

Phoenixes with their feathery wings
They shoot out fire faster than a sling
Zombies and skeletons are up at night
Vampires and werewolves get up to fight.

Leprechauns as green as lime
When ogres are getting covered in slime
Gnomes and goblins are having fun
Ghosts and ghouls are hiding from the sun.

Dire wolves and demons are howling away
Dwarfs and griffins are off to play

Giant crabs and spiders, the crabs crawling out
Going to Fantasy Land is an awesome shout.

Grace O'Neill (11)
Greenhill Primary School, Coatbridge

Chocolate Land

Chocolate Land is my land,
it's like my favourite band.
Creamy times are always the best,
every day, I eat the rest.
Ice cream comes, then is gone,
it just gets finished, done.
Chocolate bunnies hop away,
all around every day.

White chocolate is good,
people think it's rude.
The chocolate tree has fun,
when you do a really bad pun.
Almost the day when Chocolate Land becomes a city,
why is it a pity?
Everyone is ready,
but they aren't steady.

The chocolate river flows with goodness,
everybody dies inside this.

Chocolate milk is very small,
it's not even that tall.
Chocolate ice cream, nice and creamy,
it's also very dreamy,
when it's nice and steamy.

Arran MacInnes (11)
Greenhill Primary School, Coatbridge

Candy Land

Candy Land is the place to be
it's your chance to be set free.
With Skittles falling from the sky
you will think you're flying high.

With a chocolate river that never runs out
and a giant Toblerone, a sizeable amount.
Children laughing all day long
all happy, having a sing-song.

A house with candy canes
and lots of funny games.
Making buns and cakes
filled with honey and dates.

Ethan Fleming (11)
Greenhill Primary School, Coatbridge

Dad's World

My dad lives near a river,
we won't go there to slither.
We play games,
And we call each other names.

We go ice skating,
then we see a spider crawling.
We walk every day,
we also find a way.

We play Fortnite,
we go to bed at night.
We play hide-and-seek,
and we all have a peek.

Kyle Sedgeworth (11)
Greenhill Primary School, Coatbridge

Prehistoric Time

Whether it be a dodo,
or a triceratops,
it is what you will see,
from the mountaintops.

Dilophosaurus can be frustrating,
worse than raptors,
but still not as bad,
as a giganotosaurus.

An ichthyosaurus,
is just like a dolphin,
not harmful to us,
but watch your back for megalodon.

Harry Burns (11)
Greenhill Primary School, Coatbridge

My Imagination

My imagination is running wild,
because the sauce I had was very mild.

I'm imagining a chocolate river that never runs out,
and Toblerone in a really big amount.

A chocolate fish that eats real fish,
and if you cook it, it tastes nice on a dish.

So, as you can see,
my imagination is free.

Anaru Maika MacDougall (11)
Greenhill Primary School, Coatbridge

The Sports Land

T he day when I went to football,
H ard football game, very hard,
E specially hard.

S pecial sports,
P layers running,
O h, he scored a goal,
R angers are the best,
T eams, lots of teams,
S lide tackles.

L and Of Football,
A ndrew scored a goal,
N ames and numbers,
D ecided by the referee.

Andrew Stewart (8)
Harestanes Primary School, Kirkintilloch

Higiltypop

In Higiltypop
everything's top.
It's all green
and clean.
With no doubt
it's the happiest place about!

This place is so happy
because everyone is so chatty.
Come to this place
it's ace!
There is no doubt
it's the happiest place about!

The castle floats
without a moat.
The king and queen
live the dream.
There is no doubt
it's really the happiest place about!

Luke Stephen Ainsworth (10)
Helmsdale Primary School, Helmsdale

Animal Land

A dog is playing with a bone and he has to watch his tone.
N ative African animals eat all kinds of meat.
I n the forest, I see a mouse in his house.
M onkey swinging in a tree - he's hurt his knee.
A cat is fat, sitting on a mat.
L ast night, I saw a snake drinking from a lake.
S eahorses swimming in the sea - what a nice place to be.

Grace McConnach (11)
Helmsdale Primary School, Helmsdale

Unicorn And Panda Land

Every minute
of every day
is happy
in Unicorn And Panda Land.

I hear rivers
flowing happily.
I see beautiful unicorns and pandas
dancing and hopping around.
I smell cookies and cakes
being cooked in the oven.
I taste
sparkly rainbows.
I touch green green grass
and growing daisies.

I love Unicorn And Panda Land!

Danielle Cowie (10)
Helmsdale Primary School, Helmsdale

Halloween Land

The moon is full and the night's shut tight.
The witches cackle by the fire's light.
The cats are hissing by the witch's side.
While the bats are flying along the water's tide.

Pumpkins scream, "Ghosts on the prowl!"
In the distance, werewolves howl.
Vampires stomping around the street,
Waiting for their Halloween treat...

Ashli Hope (11)
Helmsdale Primary School, Helmsdale

Pillow Land

Pillows for miles and miles and miles
everyone who leaves, leaves with a smile.
Grab a blanket, you're all set
you won't want to leave, on that I bet!

I told my family I would stay for a day
I ended up staying for the whole of May!
Pillow Land is the best place to be
mainly because of the pillow tree.

Lawlyn Grant (10)
Helmsdale Primary School, Helmsdale

Unicorn And Pig Land

The unicorn's horn is shining bright
Outside on this dark, cold night.
Everyone stops and takes a glance at the gleam,
Such a vibrant light can be seen.

Pigs flying in the air
With all the candy they have to share.
Everyone sleeps on the fluffy ground
It goes completely silent, there isn't a sound.

Helen Grace Turner (11)
Helmsdale Primary School, Helmsdale

Mattress Land

My land is full of mattresses
you will soon know that it's the bounciest place
you'll have been to yet.

Each mattress has ten springs
that's all they need
to send you flying to the sky.

Mattress Land
should cost a grand
the best of all the lands.

Rhys Keith (10)
Helmsdale Primary School, Helmsdale

Candy Land

Candy Land is bright
you will see tonight
go there, you will see
candy animals roaming free.

You get yummy surprises there
like chocolate eggs and gummy bears.

Although Candy Land has no sound
there's lots to see
like the amazing marching band.

Millie Wood (10)
Helmsdale Primary School, Helmsdale

The Frosty Island

The island of ice and snow
It's been like that since a long time ago.
All the kids love snow cones
Even more than they love their phones.

Their drinks stay nice and cool
Whilst they jumped into the pool.
It snows forever and ever
And stays with that weather.

The snow is a beautiful white
And it's windy enough to fly a kite.
People always ice skate
With their best mate.

When a cough has been caught
And the water is not hot
They drink their hot drinks
Made with water from the sink.

Holly Reid (11)
Heriot Primary School, Heriot

The Land Of Sweets

In the land of sweets
There are a lot of treats
Houses made from gingerbread
Tucked up cosy in your bed.

The ocean is made of jelly
Everyone has a big belly
The lollipops are big
Bigger than a pig!

The clouds are made of marshmallow
Don't jump on them, because they're hollow
From the land, you can see the Milky Way
There are no Starbars in the way.

When the rainbow comes
Everybody says, "Yum!"
The gummy bears that live there
All have strawberry lace hair.

Daisy Hilton (11)
Heriot Primary School, Heriot

Underwater World

Every day in Underwater World,
it's wet, but I don't mind.

I hear whales wailing,
I see fish floating in the water,
I smell salty seaweed,
I taste the salty seawater,
I touch clamshells calling,
and that's the way I like it.

I hear salmon screeching,
I see clownfish trying to be cool,
I smell dead fish,
I taste the salty smell,
I touch the sea enemies,
and that's the way I *don't* like it.

Flynn Walker (10)
Heriot Primary School, Heriot

Wasteland

W andering around, you will find no one
A ll the trees and green are gone
S nakes roam the land, take care not to hurt
T errible creatures hide in the dirt
E verybody hides underground
L ight fades fast on the landfill site
A pple cores, old chairs, what a delight
N ewcomers welcome, bring your own grub
D on't get too dirty, we've not got a tub.

Aaron Willis (11)
Heriot Primary School, Heriot

Arcade World

In Arcade World
There's no copyright
Don't annoy Man-Pac, he might bite
He has an arcade machine as a home
And the cars, well, I can't describe them in this poem
The Road-Crossy Chicken high score is fourteen
Don't think anybody will beat that, old bean
The citizens that live here really stand out
Although, you don't actually see many about.

Sam Fletcher (11)
Heriot Primary School, Heriot

The Land Of Cats

In the Land Of Cats, they all wear hats
In the Land Of Cats, they all have mats
In the Land Of Cats, the supermarkets are filled with rats
In the Land Of Cats, they eat lots of rats
In the Land Of Cats, no living fish to be seen, except for in the blue sea
In the Land Of Cats, no living rats to be seen
Except for in the deepest, darkest caves ever!

Sofia Pirone (9)
Heriot Primary School, Heriot

Cat Land

Cat Land is so cool
It even has a kitty pool
You can play all day
Or you can laze away.

They have so much fun
Then they go for a run
They eat lots of cake
That their gran's make.

They play with kitty toys
The girls keep away from boys
People love a cat
And that is that.

Louella King (10)
Heriot Primary School, Heriot

Peppermint Heaven

Here in Peppermint Heaven,
the river flows by.
It's made of peppermint tea, you know,
the taste is simply divine.
But now it's time to start the rhyme,
and lead you on a tour.
Before we go, you need to know,
that everything is fine.

You can eat the grass,
you can eat the trees.
In fact, you can eat it all.
Come on and we will start the tour,
at the grand old city hall.

Everything is made of peppermint,
in case you didn't know.
From the houses to the trees,
and the grass to the river.
Yes, unicorns exist,
but we might give them a miss.

We are running out of time,
I'm getting shivers down my spine.

And now it's time for you to go,
there's one last thing you need to know.
As winter winds blow,
there is candy snow.
I'm sorry you couldn't see it all,
you're probably, really, really appalled.
But please, come back another day,
I would really like you to come and play.

Eilidh Christine Kerr (10)
High Mill Primary School, Carluke

Family Land

In Family Land, nothing is bland
The trees are split
But only a little bit
The sun is bright
Nobody comes out at night.

The family play on the beach
And they eat a lot of sweets
The children play in the sand
While Mum and Dad make a Family Land
The sandcastle is so tall
It's bigger than a beach ball!

Family Land can be your land
But only if you don't make it bland
You can come whenever you like
Don't be afraid, the children don't bite
Some say it's not fun
But don't listen, it's fine when you come along.

Becky Williamson (10)
High Mill Primary School, Carluke

Sweet Thing

In the land of sweet things,
it's always happy, joyful.
All the foods, as well as the sweets,
look so tasty here.
When you touch the clouds,
it's like touching candyfloss.
The rivers are covered in chocolate,
the stones are jawbreakers.
The ground is nice and soft feeling,
made out of marshmallows; on them are some unicorns.
The sky is so blue,
like the sea.
The unicorns are pink, fluffy,
and they love to dance on the rainbow.

Leahmarie Martin (11)
High Mill Primary School, Carluke

Crash Site

C rashed plane
R eally a pain
A nd the fact that the fire
S izzled the wine!
H ow come the plane could not go higher?

They are still alive.
Outside communication is gone.
Their phones aren't alive.
You can hear it in their tone.

S ighting a plane fly by
I n the blue sky
T hat's really a pain
E verybody's hopes aren't high.

Aiden Isik (11)
High Mill Primary School, Carluke

Nightmare Land

N o one dares to go in
I f you do, you are not brave, but stupid
G o in if you dare, but you will not come back
H uge spiders are waiting for you
T im the T-rex likes to flex
M assive snakes slither slowly around you
A massive population of vampires
R adioactive mushrooms; don't eat them
E nchanting warlocks you may see.

David Connacher (11)
High Mill Primary School, Carluke

Griffin Utopia

Look in the air,
beings in the sky.
We show them lots of care,
griffins flying on high.
They sleep in the hay,
and they eat in the sky.
I'd like to ride one today,
I wanna see if I can fly.
Griffin Utopia's a great place to be,
the perfect place for you and me.

Oliver Isik (10)
High Mill Primary School, Carluke

Summer City

S unny Summer City where every day is sunny.
U nder the sun in their sandcastle houses.
M asterpiece sandcastle homes.
M orning walks by the salty sea.
E verybody lives on the sunny, sandy beach by the sea.
R owing boats in the clear blue sea.

Jasmin Todd (11)
High Mill Primary School, Carluke

Star Wars Land

A land disguised as a ship
so no one can destroy it.

Amazing Poe Dameron flies the ship
with a tawny-brown Wookiee called Chewbacca.

They drink gold banana milkshake
slurping loudly.

Eating mint-green grass
that blows slowly.

Under the spaceship
jam-red lava dances wildly.

The sky-blue water
splashes quickly.

Rocky asteroids come into the ship
but some just connect with the ship.

The Death Star comes
Destroying the ship.

Matthew Sim (9)
Inverallochy School, Inverallochy

Fairyland

Fairies clothed in colour, flying gracefully in the air
Gigantic trees moving slowly
Tall, multicoloured houses sturdily standing
Charming, gorgeous flowers moving backwards and forwards
The honey-yellow, bright sun coming up over the houses
An enormous multicoloured rainbow beautifully appears
The mammoth meeting tree moving slowly
Pink, purple, red, blue and yellow food tempting me
All colours of beautiful fairy magic dust moving through the air.

Katie Crockett (10)
Inverallochy School, Inverallochy

Party Land!

Multicoloured party hats
joyfully dancing

Rainbow-spotted disco floor
moving to the beat

Kaleidoscopic colossal banners
swaying in the music

Midnight-black and cloudy grey speakers
shaking mentally to the music

Marble-coloured disco ball
gracefully spinning

Speckled honey-orange and punch-pink lights
shimmering brightly

Blaring disco music
blasting loudly.

Cameron Ritchie (10)
Inverallochy School, Inverallochy

Fairyland

F laming butter-yellow sun shining all the time
A rctic-blue watery waves steadily shimmering
I ndigo and hot pink sparkling nails and buttermilk-yellow skin
R ough gingerbread-brown trunks with pear-green leaves
I lluminating colossal fluffy clouds slowly swaying
E merald-green leaves and a pecan-brown trunk with multicoloured windows
S parkling rainbow fairy dust flying everywhere.

Monique Ritchie (10)
Inverallochy School, Inverallochy

Kitten Land

Spotty, fluffy cats
climbing everywhere.

A multicoloured, dazzling rainbow
appears magically.

Miniature mint-green trees
dancing in the wind.

Sparkly stars shimmering.

Pear-green grass
swaying in the wind.

Puffy, fluffy clouds
swimming in the sky.

Katie Noble (9)
Inverallochy School, Inverallochy

Cosmetic City

M agical dazzling rainbows
A flaring brown eyebrow raises
K aleidoscopic shining sparkles singing like fairies
E very fluffy, puffy feather dances with the rainbow

U p with the smooth brown eyeshadow, popping slowly
P uffy brushes with a glint of sparkle.

Emily Claire Marie Stephen (10)
Inverallochy School, Inverallochy

Minecraft Town

The huge castle standing in the town
Gigantic spaceships hovering over the city
The tiny birdcage over the water
Mammoth army boats leaving the harbour
Small people walking slowly
Shiny chains hang from the drawbridge
Tall helicopters land on the pad.

Nathan Novell-Frazer (10)
Inverallochy School, Inverallochy

Happy Land

Magnificent sunset slowly rising
Deep blue sea getting warmer
Beautiful mermaid singing beautifully on the seabed
Luxurious sunbed quickly warming up
Marvellous road with amazing cars on it
Colossal path with people using it.

Caleb Howe (10)
Inverallochy School, Inverallochy

Scary Scale City

Where dinosaurs writhe in never-ending coils
And gigantic worms slither in the soil
Huge gnarled trees fill the land
Horrifying serpents roam in the sand
Terrible, earsplitting cries echo all around
From miles off, you can hear that deafening sound
You will never know if you're predator or prey
Perhaps you'll be standing over magma at the end of the day
Massive tall leaves tower above
In this kind of land, there is no love
Daisies and flowers do not exist
Rainbows and pretty things? You wish!
An ominous feeling wafts through the night
Enormous bloodthirsty beasts give you a fright!
So think before you take a stand
And proceed in this gory, prehistoric, deadly land.

Nimrita Kaur Samra (9) & Eva Jean Stirling
The High School Of Glasgow, Bearsden

Lollipop Land

In Lollipop Land,
Nothing is bland,
Covered in colours, dark and light,
You will fall in love when you take a bite.

Gingerbread houses stand tall and proud,
Whilst lollipop children shout very loud,
Unicorns dance upon candyfloss clouds,
Little lemon bonbons chatter in crowds.

Candy cane trees shimmer in the sun,
As gummy bears have lots of fun,
Meanwhile, bubblegum blossoms on a bush,
While fairies go down rainbows saying, "Woosh!"

So find this world before it's gone,
Where you can stuff your face from dusk 'til dawn...

Maya Marshall (9) & Hannah Eve Reilly (9)
The High School Of Glasgow, Bearsden

Crushing Candy

C andy could not be better, because it is just smashing
A mazing candy canes are decorative and yummy
N othing in our Candy Land is bad
D elicious lollies are sticky and strong
Y ummy candy is the best!

Chloe Kirk (8) & Rosie Snedden
The High School Of Glasgow, Bearsden

YOUNG WRITERS INFORMATION

We hope you have enjoyed reading this book – and that you will continue to in the coming years.

If you're a young writer who enjoys reading and creative writing, or the parent of an enthusiastic poet or story writer, do visit our website **www.youngwriters.co.uk**. Here you will find free competitions, workshops and games, as well as recommended reads, a poetry glossary and our blog.

If you would like to order further copies of this book, or any of our other titles, then please give us a call or visit **www.youngwriters.co.uk**.

Young Writers
Remus House
Coltsfoot Drive
Peterborough
PE2 9BF
(01733) 890066
info@youngwriters.co.uk